In Your Crib

ESSENTIAL POETS SERIES 230

**Canada Council
for the Arts**

**Conseil des Arts
du Canada**

**ONTARIO ARTS COUNCIL
CONSEIL DES ARTS DE L'ONTARIO**

an Ontario government agency
un organisme du gouvernement de l'Ontario

Guernica Editions Inc. acknowledges the support of the Canada Council
for the Arts and the Ontario Arts Council. The Ontario Arts Council
is an agency of the Government of Ontario.

We acknowledge the financial support of the Government of Canada
through the Canada Book Fund (CBF) for our publishing activities.

In Your Crib

Austin Clarke

GUERNICA

TORONTO • BUFFALO • LANCASTER (U.K.)

2015

Michael Mirolla, general editor
Julie Roorda, editor
David Moratto, interior designer
Guernica Editions Inc.
1569 Heritage Way, Oakville, ON (CANADA) L6M 2Z7
2250 Military Road, Tonawanda, N.Y. 14150-6000 U.S.A.

Distributors:
University of Toronto Press Distribution,
5201 Dufferin Street, Toronto (ON), Canada M3H 5T8
Gazelle Book Services, White Cross Mills, High Town, Lancaster LA1 4XS U.K.

First edition.
Printed in Canada.

Legal Deposit – First Quarter
Library of Congress Catalog Card Number: 2014950183
Library and Archives Canada Cataloguing in Publication

Clarke, Austin, 1934-, author
In your crib / Austin Clarke. -- 1st edition.

(Essential poets series ; 230)
Poems.
Issued in print and electronic formats.
ISBN 978-1-77183-020-1 (pbk.).--ISBN 978-1-77183-021-8 (epub).--
ISBN 978-1-77183-022-5 (mobi)

I. Title. II. Series: Essential poets series ; 230

PS8505.L38I69 2015   C811'.54   C2014-906226-5   C2014-906227-3

In Your Crib

Do you remember when you climbed
into the shining machine, tugged the shift
to a forward gear, and went in the wrong direction,
into the freshly painted garage? The brickwork
cost you thousands, afforded from hours
sitting in the sound of jazz, playing Kings and Li'l Ones;
Coltrane and Miles and Aretha; the card table.
Miles and Aretha in moaning, tinny disdain,
the puzzling sheets of Coltrane, and the nervous drop
of bank notes crisp and trembling, dropping ...
dropping ... dropping ... dropping on the tablecloth,
oil skin instead of linen, to keep the cards silent,
and the intention hidden.

The Mercedes-Benz,
statue of wealth and beauty and geometric design:
an inverted Y? An M? Fresh
from a carwash, in this neighbourhood,
with high-powered soap sprays
like those from a gun ... you know guns.
And how fast they can travel; faster than the Benz
in third shifting gear. Bram! The grill smashed dead.
Crumpled in water-melon fragility.
I ask you. What you gonna do?
What you gonna do ...
words finding no object
or predicate.
Again! What you gonna do?

I turn my head aside
and my eyes of disregard
filled with disgust, I do not want to see,
to know, to understand.
For you are invisible to me
walking in this district, common to me and you.
I do not hear your anger walking
on the tidy squares of white cement
blocks covered with snow,
identical for me and for you.
I do not see your plight,
I do not want to hear your anger.

I cannot cut my small room in half,
to lend you a lodging for the night,
after you have smashed your only means of
        transportation
and of escape: escape from this neighbourhood,
yours and mine. And other nameless, unspeaking,
hiding neighbours, inappropriate first
at your birth: inappropriate still
at your up-and-down-bringing.

You are dressed in fashionable "rags" that fall below
    your waist
sagging your testicles, wanting warmth in this Canadian
    cold;
multicultural ice touching your heart; wanting to parade
your strength and independence, and your rights:
rights to be taken for no granted rights:
to be rendered guilty before the evidence
of your state is written down on thick pages
of the Book of Law and of custom,
and their trust in assumptions.

But we're still breathing fumes of German
        architecture:
engines and oil and symbols; with speed measured
in softness, in the near disappearance of sound;
and I stand, looking at this spectacle
and at the anger that buries your decision
to change your outfit to one that fits;
or fit your anger, to make it bright and spectacular
in these cut-down pants flopping and proclaiming
your new independence loosed, and imagined
that it is for your comfort;
unrestrained by no belt or buckle,
falling on to your knees, in benediction,
like your mother surrendering to the religion
of your black image
and of your style. Or, should you have changed
back into the tailor-made suit of black
and look like an undertaker, undertaking
a body before it is cold in the dead mud
and dirt, of everlasting silence?

No policeman should dare interrupt your "walk"
on this displayed "parade"
where style and fit are measured
in a long-lasting clapping that is your applause,
that it is your clothes that maketh the man.
No policeman shall punctuate the meaning of your
        "threads",
to test the latest style in fashionable "black".
For you need neither belt nor buckle
to keep your drawers from dropping to sweep the road,
nor the gutter, nor the cold cement of incarcerating
        stone
caught out of guard, in the new
down-pouring of rain that is colder,
and more punishing, in your new surroundings.

You see what I'm saying? You, at your stupid-acting
in the vernacular of your origin?
For your real vernacular, like the colour of your skin,
is wrapped in this environmental strangeness;
and you have chosen the wrong punctuation,
to write your history with a pen that holds no ink.
No ink of the colour to secure your passage.

My hand reaches out to grab you by the belt,
to lift you in brotherhood and brotherly-love
from the swirling cold of slippery fallen snow.
But you have lost that brown-leather strap,
the last redeeming tab of raiment.
My smile of brother and of brotherhood
was spent long ago, in the witnessing of brothers
for good and for bad, the un-dying rages
of rope, of whip, of gun, or of burial,
witnessing the dead, still stiff, and satisfied,
sinking in the ground, to turn to dust.
When I lost these tokens of allegiance
and walked away from the brink of death,
left you un-buried on the lip of the grave,
your un-buried, and un-ploughed grave
nothing was left in me but the taste
and the haste of my intention.
Money was not the problem.
There was "never no money, man!"
Bail? Or loan? Or gift? Or dividing-up
of the stolen loot.
For there were no Elders.
Only old men:
as the Poet said.
There were no Elders? None?
Only old men only.

You shall go then, into the storming winter
with no armament of friend nor guide.
The Benz shall, in a miracle of engineering,
drive you clean
into the hands
of the Law.

I have been following, from the silent rear
the deaths and burials of our Elders
cut down with their words of freedom
congested in their lips like un-played notes,
cut down from the sycamore trees in another place;
I have talked with, and walked in lines behind Malcolm X;
shared a microphone with Stokely Carmichael;
brushed shoulders and jokes with Floyd McKissick,
Roy Innis of the Urban League, and on a train
pulling out from Grand Central Station, I have
sat in the company H. Rap Brown. I have walked
in the company of "true-true" Elders:
John Henrik Clarke, with a house bulging-full of books,
under his pillow, under his bed,
like hidden treasure and booze;
LeRoi Jones, newly baptized Amiri Baraka,
leaning across the shaking club car seat,
just as I had raised one strip of sizzling
bacon to my lips, to admonish,
"Brother! Do you eat the *piggg*??"
This brother, and many more
brothers and sisters too who called themselves
"followers of the Honourable Elijah Mohammed" ...
while Malcolm X was weighing the balancing and the
        logic,
and America's choice: "the bullet or the ballot?"
Which is no choice at all.

I was in the company then, of "true-true" Elders.
And I kept silent. Then. And when Stokely said, "Hell, no!
We won't go!" ... meaning his refusal to obey the Draft;
and his refusal to fight and kill Vietnamese, I kept silent.
Then, H. Rap Brown shouted, "Vi'lence is Americman
as cherry pie!"
And Martin Luther King,
having the same dreams of freedom ...
before he was called up Yonder by a bullet ...
broke into a lullaby: " ... I have a dream!
I have a dream,
That one day soon,
that little black boys,
and little white girls,
will go to school,
together. I have a dream!
Freedom now."

There have been no Elders attending your arrests,
your questionings; your answers
scoffed at by the encircling, bracing
cuffs of shining steel, the jewels
of your new brotherhood
as Suspect, and as Black Criminal.
A "person of interest," as if you were a lover.

Is this, then, your answer to my silence –
your heedlessness, your profanity, the clicking
of your new bracelets of steel?
Your rebellion, your silence, and the silence of all
others who swear upon the Bible,
and condemn you as violent.
Because you are black?
Because it is Black History Month?
But violence has always been used in history,
and in songs, in jazz and the blues,
to make the point, not read, not heeded, not
understood – your language, your voice.

"**I** have a dream!"
This voice was used to soften
the pain of prison, and not to raise rebellion.
Words were hardly spoken then
before the guns exploded.
Give me liberty or give me death.
Liberty-less that man fell in a "brotherly" congregation
gathered and gathering close, on that brisk Sunday
     afternoon,
in the home of blackness.

"We will go back to Africa!" they said.
And in search of Africa, they all went.
And to Harlem, they all went.
And stopped. And settled. In Harlem:
the Africa of their dreams.
Elders, the old men,
mens and womens too,
was walking behind them.
Obedient, like slow-moving hearses,
with civility, like in "civil rites" parades,
in dashikis, wearing robes
that flowed to the pavement,
the same pavement,
serving now as their graves:
blown-down to the ground
by high-powered hose
and policemen's billy-clubs;
and restaurants with signs saying:
"No niggers, Jews, or dogs allowed,"
and you may not put your thick black lips
under this cool Southern nozzle, to get a drink
at the cooling fountain.

Y̲ou have not experienced this joy:
the touch of water, bathing your body clean,
the baptizing warmth, while the doves and sparrows
like growing sugar cane in the fields of blue,
in the waves, and in the ripples
and the tormenting sting of a kiss by a sea-animal;
your resurrection and baptism
wrapped in the kiss of cooling waves
shouting "haii-haii-haii ..."
Memories of bedtime stories, kneeling at the foot of
your bed of straw, at the soft white, silk cushion
in your Shakers' Tabernacle, back home
in Barbados, on Golf Club Road, at the foot
of poplar trees, and breadfruit trees,
when you were free and used to wear silk ...
swimming in the salt, sweet, soothing warm but cool
        waves
that bathed your body in that embracing peace.
The sprays of salt water were the salve
of contentment, before you substituted
that gift of nature with pools of snow
and melting ice, and some firm snow,
under the weight of galoshes, left
by the black-leather-and-rubber winter wear,
that marks your progress in the falling frozen fog
tumbling in, like waves, and like snowfall,
the hurricanes of a Canadian winter.

The weather of emigration changed your
    pronunciation
of words you did not grow up imitating, or practicing:
woman and wife became "hos"; lady labelled "bitch",
laughing-matters, disrespected.
Is this why, in years that followed,
that are following still,
you turned from father to absentee,
with your offspring,
and you became a visitor to your own "crib"
and not a tenant? Are you a bird that's lost
its sight and ownership,
flying now, low, in silent uncertainty
round the nest made soft, with sprigs and straw,
and the occasional once-in-a-birthday present,
into the nest vacated by you, in blindness?
When you abandoned it there?

For who had the most of these "bitches",
are the very ones who grew up to drive machines
'factured by Germans. Calling them "Rides".
Riding your new cock-horse, to Banbury Cross!
Your new speech did not grow out of education
in Black English, did not have its origin
in well-trained syntax that gouges out words
that best explain your disagreements.
A name was a name.
A name was a word with no declension.
It could, and was, calculated
and defined by any intention you cared
to stamp your woman with.
Or your friend with. Your Elder, if you had one, with.
Your "ace-boon-coon", with.
Your meaning was a whiff of your fags,
your "shit" your entire conversation.
You did not demand, like Aretha Franklin,
"R-e-s-p-e-c-t!"

Your lexicon is filled with new words:
your "wheels", your "piece",
your "crib", and your "brother",
but "brother" was your last breath of respect.
Love however, waited on your lips.
(Are lips not used for confession,
and making love?)
And you confessed, on the point of death;
the gun was pressed against your heart.

And now, again, I see that you lost
your Elders before you even had them.
No Elders to remind you of your age,
and the luck you were born with.
So, I must cry "Again?"
But how many times shall my "Agains"
occupy the pages of your unwritten book,
of blood-stained paper, that brings you
silent
deranged
tricked
flogged
with red letters
Xes and Vees
crossing the landscape
of your black skin?

Yes, again.
Again and again.
Watching you from a safe distance
on the second floor
before sleep and exhaustion,
before you faded into the blackness of your skin and
    intention,
calling from the third floor,
safer there in the skies, circled by iron
and security alarms;
I watched as the white van with red lettering
counting, like a child learning
the tables of discipline,
numbers stamped
on fender and on trunk:
POLICE DIVISION
"1, 2, 3 ..."
conveyance to the cell.
And when he let you go, I did not
breathe a sigh for your victory over
the portrait you faced him with:
dashiki, locks dangling in dreaded
imitation, sandals that flipped-and-flopped
under your toes and calves, moistened
by coconut oil, and other ointments
going back to Africa and the Caribbean
in piteous imitation of satisfaction;
satisfaction in this victory, leaving behind you
the curse, the favourite name you called him by,

swaggering your victory by the deep pull
on a cigarette you took from a secret
crevice of your body ...
calling him by that name.

But again: suppose I had intervened
telling the man with the red scribbles on his car
that you are my brother ...
had collected the strands of logic
and known the locked bracelets, the push,
the assault, the names practised for your
behaviour, presence, and appearance
become the same identity reserved for me.
But you would not really know,
for these things, these "incidences" are
kept under the hat, the helmet, the plastic
cap, with a number on it,
kept secret and sacred, for me, like you.

Why, again, did I never
push my way, my body, my words
beside you, and claim the allegiance
of the blood?
Why did I not, like an Elder,
rummage through my dresser and take
a pair of short pants two sizes too large
round the waist and thigh, and turn the peak of my cap ...
my College cap in which I played the gentleman's game
of cricket, and claim in gentlemanly shouts
just below the level of decency,
"hows-zatt?" And as one gentleman to another,
watch you walk, unspeaking, undoubting,
unquestioning the decision to *give you out*.

How many times have you been given out?
How many times has the ball exploded
on your pads, made of thick protecting padded cloth,
and you "walked"? And your posture
was not belligerent. How many times
when the red-and-white painted car with the spar,
the antenna, the murmuring radio
sending a Morse-code of guilt,
have you ever doubted your own innocence?

When you are stopped, driving this big shiny car
in the "wrong neighbourhood," when you
are caught "unlawfully" … God forbid that
you are caught with no hoodie on your head
or trousers sagging down below your waist …
for if your outfit matches the expectation of the man
in the ticking cruising car, you are a goner.
Whenever you trespass in a neighbourhood
where other "rich cars" are parked, you'll be judged
a suspect, casing the neighbourhood,
where colour instructs the Law
that you are trespassing.
Your presence there turns this respectable
	neighbourhood
into a ghetto. You have entered the wrong
	neighbourhood.
Where you come from is the ghetto. Remember that.
A violent neighbourhood. Remember that.
And the admission of mistaken identity
will not grant you bail. Remember that.
You shall spend the night inside a pen,
inside a crib … Remember that …
where breakers of the Law, and drivers like you,
who are lost, breakers of the prevailing definition of the
	Law,
shall reinforce your guilt.
And you who have argued, and still do argue,
and who have lived with the argument,

"Toronto is a multicultural town"; white and black and
     brown
live in multitudinous-multicultural harmony,
the truth that defines this society is
that if you are black
you are a speck
on the mixed-cultural landscape.
You will learn, in fast time, or in retarded time
that there is a different ruler
that measures how the Law fits your body,
as a shirt that is measured erroneously
fits the wrong pattern.

Elder-less, this ditty's
never touched your ears:
"if you are white,
you're right.
If you are brown,
You can stick around.
But if you are black,
get a wa-a-ay back!"
Its warning was composed years
before you were born in Africa, or in the West Indies too.
But you heard multicultural words
as a welcoming permission. Permission
coloured your vision, pernicious smile of entry.
Again ...

For there are no Elders.
Only old men standing
in disregard.
Old men, we shall go
to everlasting dampness
in the grave, buried deeper
in everlasting silence.
Silence my words and the description
with which I opened this confession:
your castigation,
unrecognizable to you.

How many times, nevertheless,
shall I bend at the waist,
with my hands in the soiled water
in an enamel basin, scabbed
with the eczema of black caking dots,
and apologize? My eyes did not see your black skin,
your skin was invisible
under the glare of your nearness,
of your presence, of your habitation,
on a community playground, in silent
uneasy residence
when the sun goes down.
You know, that with suns,
sometimes too with moons,
always with wind and storm,
hurricanes and the winds of speculation
that blow uncertain, this tribulation
covers your head; and you know too, that people
cannot see in this thick racial darkness.

Again? Yes! Again, in your crib ...
Your thirst for justice,
and your presumptions of being loved
disappear like the snow
and the blistering wind,
disappear in the month of May.
Warm days and nights that lurk
in your neighbourhood with the patience
of white limousines, and of Job,
red numerals painted on them,
hardly breathing panthers trained
to pounce and count their hopes
of catching you. You've been caught.
Had.
Convicted.
The unproven nature of crime,
of disturbance,
of silence,
of misunderstanding.
Misunderstanding is known by all the other residents
in the lie of this multicultural land
in which you chose,
like a poor man chooses
the ticket, every Friday night,
to make a fortune
from the Lottery's spinning-wheel
that plays for luck.
"Fall on your knees."
If you had, as custom tells you

that you have, four knees,
you would resemble that animal
that you are described to be.
The two legs that you walk on,
are the gifts of the thoughts of your society,
the society that has circumscribed you
with those very thoughts.

There is no redemption for a man,
black or white, who lugs his "piece"
into the sacred stalls at a funeral,
when his "piece", that passeth all understanding,
presses soft against his conscience,
his "piece" of death
when he is seeking this peace.
All the funerals that you attend, all the songs ...
are they songs of everlasting grief?
Are they songs of redemption?
Are they songs of old grief,
that ask for understanding?
Or are they songs of forgiveness?
"How sweet the name of Jesus sounds in a believer's
      ear?"
"Amazing Grace?"
"The day Thou gaveth, Lord, is ended?"
"Nearer my God, to Thee?"
Or, is it any one ballad by Bob Marley,
documenting sea captains that
"rob I ... sold I to the merchant ships ..."

Your birthday party
where you take the cake.
Explosions,
not balloons filled with water.
Not crackers. Nor jerk pork,
heavy-sweets, vodka and cognac.
(No more rum-and-coke.
For you are, now, a man with class.)
Your killing, your death, your existence, and your reward
are guns: guns are the trophy of your existence;
guns aimed, then kissed, then pointed,
then fired. From your hand,
at burial ceremonies, and the lowering
of coffins, the pouring of drinks,
celebrations for weddings
and birthdays; parties ... and you have
a word for these celebrations ... which shall remain
lying in no expression.
You do not talk to the cops to give them
names and intentions, fodder
for their guns and sprays, and other things
that "old pirates" walk with
and that are trained to empty into the beauty
of your black, shivering skin.

You have this tired, old Elder
singing the blues, mouthing
"... and we shall overcome
... someday" ... watching you from
my distance, invisible to you,
as you climb the ladder
to success and suicide,
silently rapping you not to forget
the words of your true-true brother,
Bob Marley, pleading, wailing, painting your past,
in words that tell you of the history of this verse,
telling you once more, again and again,
that this present lies in your history.
Is your history.
"Old pirates, yes
they rob I;
sold I to the merchant ships ..."

"Yes!"
But we, the old men
wallowed in the immorality of our silence.
We remained silent, in our tentative successes,
in universities, teaching new dogs old tricks,
achieving tentative acclamation
that we had made something of ourselves:
our lives of acknowledged distance
from the black communities,
glorying in moderation.
Success is measured by where we live,
where we take our vengeance on our brothers,
where we renounce these Elders and call them
old men, outliving their relevance,
as they keep their distance,
and the role models amongst us.
We have lived to our own music, discordant
to your native beat and rhythm,
it confuses us,
trained to listen
to a different beat
and drummer.
And here am I, critic of your struggle to live,
live barricaded inside your own "community",
a ghetto not of physical dimension.

Again? Again. And again.
Old as the pirates in Bob Marley's anthem,
old as the history of marching and singing
songs of freedom, and doing the latest jig,
the Boogaloo, the Funky Chicken, the latest movement
of waist and behind, to beat: Aretha and Abbey Lincoln
and men who sing the Blues ...

Do not follow the pattern of your exclusion,
thinking you have given this country nothing.
You have given more than they are ever able,
or wish, to recompense you for.
Rap! Painting the face of this country's youth,
and understanding, in small measure,
the properness of rhyme, and rebellion
contained in the un-rhyming words,
pelted with the speed of bullets, into your faces,
into their new eager sympathy for ghetto,
guns, secrets, and mouths shut tight
against the false evidence of "persons of interest":
your neighbours in black communities, who are black.
But as the rappers sing, you live in fear of obedience.
Your own trepidation of obeying Commandments:
including "Thou shalt not bear false-witness."

We, Elders, or old men, or both,
have bathed ourselves in the immorality of loud silence,
and we go to everlasting silence greater
than the one living underneath the fig trees
in a cathedral's yard, with the wind touching
our coffins, like lips found finally, in their farewell.

But, before I go, slow, downstairs,
as if I am riding in an elevator, so silent
that I have forgotten if it has wheels, in silence
let me now, as an old man,
rest my heavy, last request:
listen.

I am a man, old of age and disappointment
for the years that passed me by, and wanting company.
I invited you in, and tried to live with you,
real and lasting; but you have been outliving me,
testing the horror-scope of my life,
and the lens I saw you through. For there was no
bungalow, and no elders in Mississauga,
when I was conceiving a father-figure for you,
after your mother had already conceived you,
in the same lack of focus, and of faith.
My silence, immoral or otherwise, does not
imagine you in any description
that is thrown upon your community.
The Elders say there is no community, unless
they are counting houses and street-corners,
and black faces, faces that are black,
a "black community."

So, sing your Rap.
Wear your trousers inches below the button of decency.
Cover your head, as other religions do
with a cloth of silk, cotton, or muslin material.
And forget thee not thy Hoodie,
though men, and boys, have had their bodies pierced;
by guns that kept the community safe
from guns
by men
wearing guns.
Shot dead.
Been had.
Shot dead.
Boom-boom! ... boom!
War has been declared.
Is it religious?
Racial?
Or rebellious?
From wearing this badge, of Youth?
And youthfulness?

The face is not "identical" enough, cannot be seen
or recognized, so you might beat the rap
for loitering, the precursor to theft,
or murder, or rape.
So, take the risk.
Men take risks.
Boys dream of what to risk,
when playing Kings and Li'l Ones.
Go, then, and write a black poem.
Amiri Baraka told you so – and how.
"We want a black poem. And a
Black World."
Let the world be a Black Poem
And Let All Black People Speak
          This Poem
          Silently
Or LOUD.

I do not have the gift of words
put down in certain rhyme and rhythm,
to guide your hand.
But your spirit, like your blood,
runs deep, through my veins.

The question, "Again?" that I have asked you,
in breaking my silence, redeeming my conscience,
was a question that should have graced my lips
many years before. Redemption. Redemption.
It is the word for bravery despite fear on your lips
and your trembling hand, to ask.
And since there are no Elders,
the question came from my lips and not my heart,
unaccustomed to giving advice,
good example in my voice raised high above
the stunted prophesies
written in books on religion and sociology.

Again! The first word uttered to a child,
for mis-demeanours. What man, therefore,
unless he has grown backwards, and is stunted,
would accept this diminution? Again?
But remember that I do not ask for your compassion.
Not even for your understanding.
And I do not bend my back, or my conscience
with pity.
I shall have this discussion, face-to-face, with God
whose heart is larger and much softer
than your compassion.

And in the stream of blood, thicker than water,
there are creatures of life, sticking to my flesh
sharks,
dolphins, and barracudas that are also
the population of the deep.
The deep.
The deepness.
The danger.
If I could escape the stormy water of the sea,
if I could climb back out from the soft, silk, sashes
of love and final greeting that ties and decorates
their love of me, wrapped in final affection,
and hide amongst the ridges of hills and valleys
of the silken black-and-brown bed
that Elders have decorated my going-away in,
then, at this moment of final departure,
and greater silence into the black earth,
frightening as a death;
I cannot carry with me the words and the songs,
and the dreams
I threw away.
My neglect is so cruel, unforgivable
as in ancient times, when "old pirates, yes,
they rob I" ... yes, you and I.

Others have been given house-arrest, probation,
dismissal, bail, a slap across the wrists
for offences of greater juridical disposition.
But they clothed the misdemeanour you were alleged
to have committed with the weight of the Law.
So, even if I had adorned my words
in the language of love, I could not guarantee acquittal.
And as an old man, without the certificate of
rights and of wrongs, my puny words,
if they had ever left my mouth
and were heard in the quiet, dust-ridden court
of this country's Law, nothing in my past,
nothing in my future,
nothing in my present,
could have soothed the heavy
Book of Law.

And have you, in the turmoil and regret
of life, in these streets of suburban Toronto
and Canada, have you ever permitted your thoughts
to wonder ... indeed to even wander ...
asking yourself the question:
"Is there one Book of Law for me to write
my Catechism in?"
And one for them?
Defining "them" through the eyes
and ears of your experience ...

Your closeness, and your confidence in the closeness
of experience, habit, and similarity to neighbours;
on both sides of the wire fence between your homes,
or walking the sidewalks that do not divide your
    ambition,
or your hope, success matched by joint-loyalty:
to justice, love and enjoyment. You singing Rap,
them singing the Blues.
Divided and joined at the same going-to-work bus and
    subway;
returning when dusk has gathered, like your neighbours
peeping through the blinds and windows, and dusks,
to see if neighbourliness is contagious
like the summer influenza
or the winter blues?

And you, leaderless, guided only by my silence
mixed with the two-timing urgency of dusk,
must walk this next journey, by yourself:
with no Elder, no old man, even.
Alone. No wisdom
falling out of the skies and the Heavens
to guide you ... one of the three Wise Men
in the cold night, with a slice of water melon
in its first quarter ... travelling
to Bethlehem, or Barbados.
There are many Bethlehems in our days,
bestowing myrrh and myth ...
And one of the three Kings, is black. ...

The suddenness in the changing of the colour,
the luscious green of spring and summer,
and putting on of an overcoat of golden leaves
fallen from the maturity of growth and old age.
Look up; send your glance to the apex of the limbs;
and see the silent declaration in the swifted-up
    expulsion:
the children of the maples, as you count
the days in your life, will pass through
before summer and light, and love, and you shall walk
on the same threading buds and flowers
bursting through the rectangular cement squares
you hop from, like in the game of scotch,
exclaiming in a new joy and wonder,
that you are now, living amongst neighbours
who see only, the colour of your heart.

About the Author

Winner of the Giller, Commonwealth, and Trillium Prizes for his novel *The Polished Hoe,* Toronto's Austin Clarke has published ten novels, six short-story collections, three memoirs, and one poetry collection. Among his other awards: the Rogers Communications Writers' Development Trust Prize for Fiction for *The Origin of Waves*; a Toronto Arts Award for Lifetime Achievement in Literature; the Martin Luther King Junior Award for Excellence in Writing; and a $10,000 Harbourfront Award. In 1998 he was invested with the Order of Canada. In 2003 he had a private audience with Queen Elisabeth in honour of his Commonwealth Prize. *In Your Crib* marks his second poetry collection, following 2013's *Where The Sun Shines Best*, also published with Guernica Editions.